TAMWORTH and DISTR

A Portrait in Old Picture Postcards

by
Roy Lewis

S.B. Publications

This book is dedicated to Robin, Mandy, Eleanor and Rowena Lewis

First published in 1994 by S.B. Publications
c /o 19 Grove Road, Seaford, East Sussex BN25 1TP

ISBN: 1.85770.068.6

Typeset, printed and bound by
Manchester Free Press
Longford Trading Estate, Thomas Street, Stretford, Manchester M32 0JT.

CONTENTS

By the same author in this series (A Portrait in Old Picture Postcards):

Stafford and District

Stone and District

The Haywoods

S.B.Publications also publish a wise range of local titles on Staffordshire and other areas of the country.

For details please write (enclosing S.A.E) to:-

S.B.Publications,

$^{c}/o$ 19 Grove Road,

Seaford,

East Sussex,

BN25 1TP.

INTRODUCTION

This book reproduces 88 postcards of Tamworth and District almost all from the years 1900-40. The cards are arranged as a topographical tour. The reader is invited to start in Market Street and George Street and then to look successively at Victoria Road, Bolebridge Street and Bolehall, and Colehill and Gungate. From Upper Gungate the reader turns back via Aldergate to Church Street and then to the Castle and its Pleasure Grounds. Finally comes an outer circle starting from Drayton Manor and encircling the town centre in an anti-clockwise direction taking in Fazeley, Wilnecote, Glascote, Amington, Wigginton and Hopwas.

Picture postcards were introduced into this country in 1894, exactly a hundred years before the publication of this book. Until 1902 the Post Office allowed the address alone on one side, with both a small picture and the message space on the other. The earliest postcards with views of Tamworth and Drayton Manor date from about 1900 and have pictures only half the size of the card.

From 1902 the message was allowed on the same side as the address, leaving the whole of the other side free for a picture. From this time in Tamworth, as in the rest of Great Britain, the number and variety of postcards on sale increased rapidly. By 1904 Tamworth shops were selling sets of local views published by national postcard publishers such as Stewart & Woolf of Hatton Garden, London; Valentine and Son of Dundee; and John Walker & Co of London whose trademark of a red anchor appears on some of the earliest postcards of the town.

There were also cards published by local shopkeepers. William Thomas Carrick, who had taken over the George Street stationery shop of Daniel Addison, the founder of the Tamworth Herald, began to publish postcards in 1903. His example was soon followed by Henry Green, tobacconist, in Market Street; Sally Bartle, newsagent, in Church Street; Woodcock & Son, printers and stationers, in Bolebridge Street; Charles Young, newsagent, in Victoria Road, and others.

Local photographers had probably taken most of the views used to produce these cards. They also published their own cards. The most prolific of these was C.E. Weale. Charles Weale, a chartered accountant obsessed with photography, had opened a studio at Nuneaton in the 1870's. About 1884 he moved to 23 Victoria Road, Tamworth, and rapidly became the town's leading photographer. In 1903 he began to go blind and his son Albert, who had been planning a photographic studio in Durban, returned from South Africa to take over his father's business. Almost as soon as he returned he began to produce postcards of Tamworth and district using the studio name "C.E. Weale", although all the photographs were taken by Albert or his sister Jessie. The Weales were family friends of the Woodcocks and supplied all their early postcards.

Within a few years other photographers followed Weale. A.W. Mills of Lichfield and Brownhills took many photographs of Drayton, Glascote and Wilnecote; A. Coulson of West Bromwich took a series of photographs of Drayton Manor; and, a little later, Livinia Adkin, whose family kept a newsagents shop in Fazeley, produced photographic cards of that place. The ten years from 1904 to 1914 saw a flood of postcards showing Tamworth and district. After that the number of cards steadily declined although several very interesting series were published by national companies in the 1920's and 1930's,

In 1900 Tamworth, a comparatively small but busy market town of about 7,000 people, was surrounded by rural villages such as Hopwas, Amington, and Wigginton, and industrial settlements such as Glascote with its iron foundry and glazed stoneware pipe works, Wilnecote with its colliery and brick and tile works; and Fazeley with its textile mills and breweries. The postcards reproduced here show the district as it was in the years before 1914, and some of the changes and rebuilding that had taken place before 1940. Postcard publishers did not produce cards showing the industrial side of the district or some of the lesser streets in Tamworth. This book includes as wide a selection as possible of the views that were published.

Postcards are difficult to date since publication is sometimes years later than the photograph on which the card is based. Dates given in the book are best guesses arrived at by a mixture of internal evidence, postmark date where a card has been postally used, and a study of postcard publishers.

All the postcards are reproduced from the Lewis collection except pages 15, 17, 26, 27, 28, 41, 50, 54, 64, 69 and 79 which are reproduced by permission of the Curator, Tamworth Castle, from the photographic collection in the museum.

In putting together this book I have been helped by many people who have recalled scenes on the cards, by librarians who have found books and historians who have made available the results of their own inquiries. I am particularly indebted to Mr R. Sulima, Assistant Curator at Tamworth Castle, not only for his local knowledge but also for his guidance in using the Castle's photographic collection. To all of them I record my grateful thanks. They have made the writing of this book a journey of discovery and pleasure which I hope the reader will share with me.

Roy Lewis

TAMWORTH BOROUGH ARMS, 1904
This postcard shows the seal of Tamworth
Corporation with the fleur-de-lis which has
been their badge since Tudor times. The fleur-
de-lis on a shield supported by mermaids was
accepted as the Borough coat of arms until
1936 when it was discovered that it was being
used without authorisation. Nevertheless, the
arms continued in use until the present coat of
arms was granted in 1968.

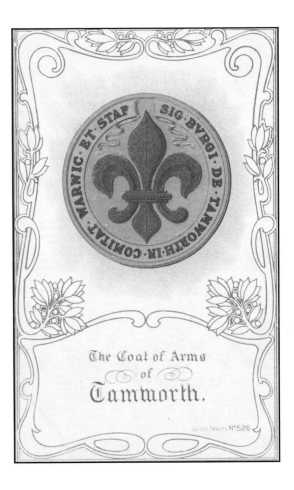

MARKET STREET, TAMWORTH, 1904

On this postcard The Peel Arms is on the left and the Castle Hotel on the right. The sign shows that the Castle Hotel was also the Midland Railway Parcel Receiving Office. This end of Market Street had a number of solid Victorian buildings some of which still exist.

MARKET STREET, TAMWORTH, 1925

Market Street is seen here on a busy Saturday in 1925 with stalls overflowing down the centre of the street. Most of the buildings are still recognizable although much altered on the ground floor. The Market Vaults is prominent on the left. Morton's boot and shoe shop (now Gemini Sports) and Felton Bros' drapery shop can be picked out on the right.

3

THE TOWN HALL AND PEEL STATUE, c1924

The Town Hall was a gift to the town in 1701 by Thomas Guy, one of the town's M.P.s, whose mother had been born in Tamworth and brought her son to live there when he was eight years old. The town stocks and pillory once stood in front of it. Since 1852 that space has been occupied by the statue of Sir Robert Peel, Prime Minister and M.P. for Tamworth. On the left the Coalville and Measham bus is waiting for passengers. Note its starting handle.

THE BUTTER MARKET, TAMWORTH, 1925

The Town Hall was built on 18 pillars to provide space under it for a covered market where butter and eggs could be sold by farmers' wives from the neighbourhood. For many years the space under the Town Hall also housed the town fire engine. The original entrance was a flight of steps leading to a balcony at the end of the building furthest from Peel's statue. These were taken down when the building was extended in the nineteenth century.

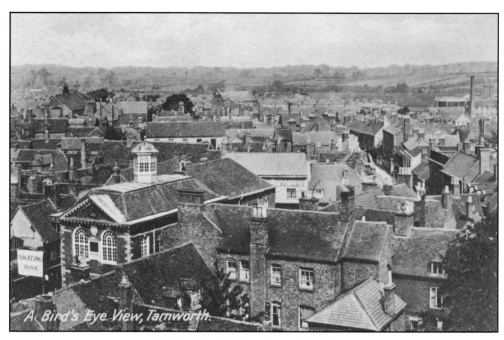

A BIRD'S EYE VIEW OF TAMWORTH, 1912

This view was taken from the roof of Tamworth Castle. The Town Hall with its roof lantern is on the left. The change in roof line between the original building and the nineteenth century extension is clearly visible. George Street curves away on the right and the gasworks can be seen in the distance. To the left of the Town Hall a hanging sign advertises the short lived roller skating rink - a pre 1914 craze - where "First Choice" is today.

6

TAMWORTH ROLLER SKATING RINK, 1912

This postcard shows the interior of the roller skating rink. In the years before 1914 almost every town had a rink with resident instructors and exhibitions of figure, fancy and trick skating. The back of this card advertises the three daily sessions of the Tamworth Rink - 10.30 to 12.30, 2.30 to 5.00 and 6.30 to 10.00pm.

GEORGE STREET, TAMWORTH, 1904

This postcard and the one on the opposite page both show the western end of George Street looking towards Market Street. On the right, in 1904, were the shops of Thomas Cope, tailor; George Griffin, watchmaker; William Prince, ironmonger; and William Carrick, stationer. Only Carrick's shop remains today. This business, started by Daniel Addison the founder of the Tamworth Herald, had been sold to Carrick in 1886. In 1904 it sold everything from newspapers to Bibles and had a good selection of local postcards like the one reproduced here.

GEORGE STREET, TAMWORTH, 1932

A similar view to that on the opposite page but taken almost thirty years later. The most obvious changes are the new Bank Building (now the Halifax Building Society) at the end of the street and the Grand Cinema, opened in 1905, with its distinctive statue on the roof. In the foreground are Pearks Stores (now Eye Care), LCM Co. Ltd (London Central Meat Company Ltd) and the curiously named "Sit Tight" shop.

GEORGE STREET, TAMWORTH, 1905

A view of George Street photographed from the bottom of Colehill in 1905. On the left is the old Post Office "open from 8am to 7.30pm for the sale of stamps and other business". The three storied building with ornate first floor windows on the right is occupied by Thomas Vaughan who carried on a thriving business in good second hand clothing. Today it houses Halifax Property Services. Note the street cleaners with spade and broom.

10

J. FRISBY, GEORGE STREET, TAMWORTH

Joseph Frisby opened his boot store at 7 George Street about 1900. His shop can be seen on the left hand side of the street in the view on page 10. Frisby sold high quality boots and provided a service to match. Before 1914 his customers were given copies of the card reproduced here. On the back is printed "Please send your assistant round for some repairs to...". Alas, the days when a shop assistant would call to collect your boots for repair are long past. Today Curry's is at Number 7.

"GOOD MORNING," *Madge, you don't look happy!*

Madge (in gig): No, my wretched boots hurt me, I've just had them repaired.

BUT SURELY you knew that **FRISBY'S** *Repaired Boots, and made them almost like new—mine have been done there and are very comfortable and look so smart.*

MORAL :

Always send your Repairs to **FRISBY'S**.

J. FRISBY, HIGH-CLASS BOOTMAKER AND REPAIRER,

7, GEORGE STREET, TAMWORTH.

GEORGE STREET, TAMWORTH, 1910

George Street as shown on this postcard is almost unrecognizable today. Many of the buildings were swept away in the 1960s and 1970s although on the right Lloyds Bank has remained unchanged. Next door is Thorburn's Boot and Shoe Warehouse with its frontage illuminated by fairy lights. In 1936 this was replaced by the present Burton's shop. On the opposite side of the road are the Town Vaults, later to be named Oliver's Hotel after the proprietor, Oliver Boonham.

12

VICTORIA ROAD FROM WEST, TAMWORTH.

COPYRIGHT TWH. 13.

LILYWHITE LTD.,
THE PHOTO PRINTERS

VICTORIA ROAD FROM THE WEST, TAMWORTH, 1925

This postcard shows Victoria Road with Heath's footwear shop on the left and Deeley & Son's bakery on the right. Both buildings still stand but with much altered windows. Victoria Road was no more than a lane leading to Tamworth Station until 1843 when it was announced that Queen Victoria was to visit Tamworth by rail. There were hasty improvements. On 15th November 1843 the Queen drove along the road named in her honour under triumphal arches and evergreen garlands.

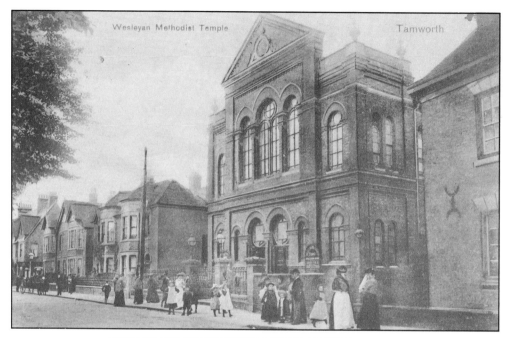

WESLEYAN METHODIST TEMPLE, TAMWORTH, 1905

The Wesleyan Methodists built The Temple in Victoria Road in 1877 to replace their old chapel in Bolebridge Street. Rooms for a sunday school were added in the following year. At the topping out ceremony when The Temple was finished, the choir ascended to the roof where they sang hymns and finished with a triumphant Hallelujah Chorus. The building ceased to be used as a church in the 1970s and is now the Victoria Club.

VICTORIA ROAD, TAMWORTH, 1925

In this view of Victoria Road, Albion Street is on the left with John Marriott's clothing shop on the corner. Two houses beyond the shop was the home and studio of Albert Weale, the formost photographer in the town and the publisher of many of the postcards in this book. The iron canopy on the right belonged to Cheetham's mineral water factory.

TAMWORTH RAILWAY STATION, 1905

At Tamworth two railways crossed. The Birmingham and Derby Junction Railway opened their station in 1839 and later became part of the Midland Railway. Their booking hall is on the right in this postcard. The Trent Valley line, built in 1847 on a lower level, used the same station but on a different level because the lines did not meet. Note the horse drawn cabs waiting for the next train to arrive. The rather splendid red brick building shown on this postcard was demolished in the 1960's when the line was electrified.

BUFFET AT TAMWORTH STATION, 1918

Tamworth Ladies Working League opened this buffet at Tamworth Station, where volunteers served tea and sandwiches to soldiers coming home on leave and those awaiting connections, from 8pm until 4am. The photograph, taken about 1918 on the London & North Western Railway platform, shows some of the volunteers with their union jack bedecked urns, teapots, cups and sandwiches.

FLOODS IN BOLEBRIDGE STREET, TAMWORTH, 1910

This part of Bolebridge Street, with Mill Lane and Gas Lane on the right, was known as the Knob. Being low lying and close to both the Tame and the Anker, it flooded regularly. This photograph, taken about 1910, shows a horse and cart providing a ferry service for cyclists and pedestrians. The water has also attracted children to watch and paddle. Note on the left the shop signs - umbrellas, a barber's pole, and the fish hung from a line outside Jehu Wilkins' fishmonger's shop.

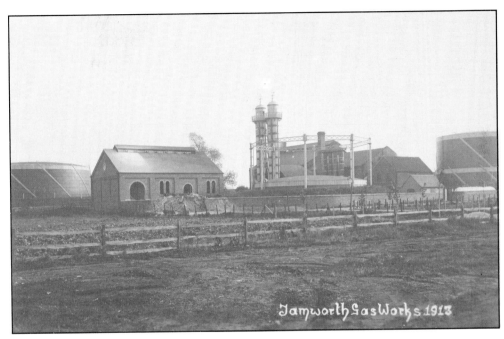

TAMWORTH GAS WORKS, 1913

Tamworth Gasworks was established in 1835 by subscription of the inhabitants with Sir Robert Peel as the largest subscriber. This postcard view of the works and the gas holders at the back of Bolebridge Street was used as a Christmas card by the Gas Company in 1913.

BOLEBRIDGE, TAMWORTH, 1910

The old narrow stone bridge across the Anker with its 12 picturesque arches was replaced in 1877 by the unlovely cast iron bridge with pedestrian walkways on either side seen in the centre of this postcard. In 1936 this, too was replaced by a steel and concrete bridge which lasted until the big "egg" round-about was constructed in the 1980s. In the background is the viaduct built in 1839 to carry the Birmingham & Derby Junction Railway across both the river and the road.

BOLEHALL ARCH, 1925

The builders of the Birmingham and Derby Junction Railway solved the problem of crossing the valley of the Anker by building a massive viaduct. There were 18 arches each 30 feet wide, one of which is shown here, and one slewed arch of twice that width. On 5 August 1839 the first locomotive, appropriately named "Tamworth", carried railway directors and local gentry across in six carriages with footmen perched fore and aft like horse drawn coaches.

TAMWORTH FROM BOLEHALL VIADUCT 1910
This view from the top of Bolehall Viaduct shows the cast iron bridge over the River Anker in the foreground.
The scene was transformed when a new road system was build in the 1980's.

TAMWORTH FROM THE RIVER ANKER, 1909

The Castle and the bandstand in the pleasure gardens can be seen on the left in the distance. The mill at the back of George Street is in the centre. The two girls in the distance standing in the middle of the river show how shallow the Anker was at that point.

COLEHILL, TAMWORTH, 1932

On the left is Dodd's drapery and millinery shop, then the Cooperative Society premises with a Hovis bread van outside, and beyond that the old vicarage iof St Editha's. The Cooperative Society, established by Rev. William MacGregor in 1886, has since extended and rebuilt its premises. The old vicarage became a milk bar and the only reminder of its past is a chuckling ghost said to be heard on the first floor. The Baptist Tabernacle can be seen at the top of Colehill.

THE BAPTIST TABERNACLE, TAMWORTH, 1912

The Tabernacle was built as a theatre where great actresses like Sarah Siddons could perform for the people of Tamworth. In 1829 the theatre had decayed and become "a shabby, ruinous pile of brick". Sir Robert Peel turned it into a malthouse and then gave it to the Baptists. After refurbishment, it was opened as The Tabernacle in 1870. In 1970, when the Baptists moved to Belgrave, the building became the Arts Centre. Rev. Donald Fraser, whose portrait is on the card, served as a chaplain in the 1914-18 War and was killed in action in France.

CASTLE CYCLE WORKS, LOWER GUNGATE, TAMWORTH, 1905

The Castle Cycle Works opened about 1890 at 50 Lower Gungate and made cycles and motor cycles for the next 40 years. This photograph of the interior of the works was taken about 1905 and shows the proprietor, William Griffiths, and his brother on the left facing the camera. The machinery is being driven from overhead belts and pulleys. Note the tricycle in the foreground with a curious basket at the front and the motor cycle behind it with a belt drive to the back wheel.

THE SCHOOLS, SPINNING SCHOOL LANE, TAMWORTH, 1921

The girls and infants schools in Spinning School Lane were opened in 1870. This postcard shows Harvest Festival in the infants' hall in 1921. The staff are lined up at the back behind the children and the produce laid out on tables. The typical high windows stopped pupils being distracted by whatever was going on outside.

JAMES EADIE LTD, ALBERT ROAD, TAMWORTH, 1900

James Eadie Ltd were Burton-on-Trent brewers, wine and spirit merchants. This photograph shows their Tamworth Stores in Albert Road near its junction with Gungate about 1900. Three horse drawn brewer's drays are also in the picture. The house to the left of the Stores was the home of Mr and Mrs Thorn who are standing with their daughter outside the house.

THE COTTAGE HOSPITAL, TAMWORTH, 1904

Tamworth Hospital was built by Rev William MacGregor in 1880. It was supported by public subscription and patients who could afford to do so paid for their treatment. At first it was a single storied building with six beds and a single nurse. A second storey was added in 1882 and the Hutton Wing, on the left in this picture, added by Mrs Hutton of Dosthill in memory of her husband in 1889. By 1904 there were 27 beds and 5 nurses. In the same year the word Cottage was dropped from its title as no longer being appropriate.

THE HUTTON FOUNTAIN, 1908

Mrs Hutton also donated this drinking fountain in memory of her husband. It was erected on a piece of land at the junction of the Ashby and Comberford roads known as The Hand. There were three drinking troughs, one for people, one for dogs, and one for horses. The inscription read "I was thirsty and ye gave me to drink". It was temporarily removed in the 1960's but has now been replaced.

TAMWORTH GRAMMAR SCHOOL, 1908

Tamworth Boys' Grammar School moved to this site on the Ashby Road in 1868. In the 1890's the school did not flourish and in 1900 Thomas Barford was appointed Headmaster to revive the school. An ex-pupil remembered him as "a man of strict morals and firm discipline". Under Barford's guidance the school grew. Its first science laboratory was built in 1904, a gymnasium and art room in 1910. In this view the Headmaster's house is at the rear and housed 20 boarders who were unable to travel home every evening. The school is now Queen Elizabeth Mercian High School.

TAMWORTH GIRLS' HIGH SCHOOL, THE KINDERGARTEN

The Girls High School began in 1905 as a joint Warwickshire-Staffordshire School in College Lane. In 1910 Warwickshire built a new school outside Tamworth and in 1913 the rest of the school moved into new premises in Salters Lane. Although built for older girls, the school also had a junior department for both boys and girls aged 5 to 10. This postcard shows the Kindergarten classes, aged 5 to 8, who were taught in a double room with a folding partition. In 1959 the School became part of Queen Elizabeth's Grammar School. The building new houses Marmion Junior School.

ST. JOHN THE BAPTIST ROMAN CATHOLIC CHURCH, TAMWORTH, 1908

This Roman Catholic Church was opened in 1829 and its first priest, Father Kelly, is buried in its small churchyard. In this 1908 postcard the Presbytery is to the left of the church and the schools to the right. Two years later a new presbytery was bought on the opposite side of the street. In 1929, to mark the church's centenary, a statue of St John was erected on the gable of the church. In 1954 the building was restored and its appearance altered.

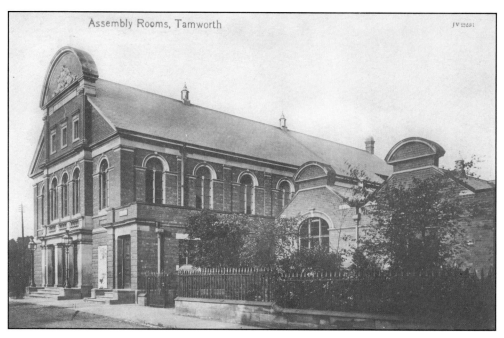
Assembly Rooms, Tamworth

THE ASSEMBLY ROOMS, TAMWORTH, 1905

The Assembly Rooms were built by public subscription in 1889 to commemorate Queen Victoria's Golden Jubilee. They provided for travelling theatres, local choirs, balls and receptions. In 1924 the Duke of York lunched here when he came to unveil the town War Memorial. In 1936 the Jarrow marchers were fed here. In 1939 it became the Civil Defence Headquarters for the town. In the words of a local reporter, "What would Tamworth do without the Assembly Rooms?"

TAMWORTH FREE LIBRARY, 1909

In 1905 Andrew Carnegie, an American millionaire who had helped establish libraries in many towns, gave a donation of £2,000 towards building this library and reading room in Corporation Street. It replaced an earlier town library in Church Street. In 1973 the library was moved to its present site and the building shown on this postcard became the Carnegie Centre.

OX ROASTING, TAMWORTH MILLENARY, 1913

In July 1913, as part of the Tamworth Millenary celebrations, the ancient custom of ox roasting was revived. The roasting took place on land in Corporation Street. It was supervised by Mr R. Wimperis (on the right) assisted by a chef from Stratford-on-Avon. Well known townspeople paid for the novelty of basting the ox and the money raised was used to provide meat for the poor. This photograph was taken just before carving began at noon.

CHURCH STREET, TAMWORTH,
1909

This postcard shows the north side of Church Street with Corporation Street on the left. Also on the left is the old Police Station, now the Social Services Area Office. This side of the road has changed less than the southern side where a large number of buildings were demolished when the new shopping precinct was built in the 1960's.

Church Street, Tamworth.

THE PARISH CHURCH, TAMWORTH, 1938

The fourteenth century tower of St Editha's Church dominates this bird's eye view of Church Street. When the tower was built it was intended to carry a spire and the base can be seen on this postcard. However, the south-east corner of the tower (on the left in this postcard) showed signs of settlement so the spire was abandoned and pinnacles built at each corner of the tower. Today the demolition of nearby buildings has opened out the view of the Church.

THE BATHS AND INSTITUTE, CHURCH STREET, TAMWORTH, 1904

This postcard shows the medieval building known as "The Paregoric Shop", famous for its sweets, on the right. Next to it is the Public Baths and Institute opened by the Rev. William MacGregor in 1885 and presented by him to the Co-operative Society. In winter the swimming bath was boarded over and became a ballroom where popular dances were held. The Art School also held its classes here. The building was pulled down in 1968 to make way for the new Co-operative Society Stores.

LICHFIELD STREET, TAMWORTH, 1907

On the left is the Peel School built in 1851 to replace an older building on the opposite side of the road. In his lifetime Sir Robert Peel provided each of the 100 scholars with a loaf of bread each week and a uniform consisting of a peaked cap and a brown velveteen coat decorated with buttons bearing the Peel family crest. By 1907 the building had been converted into Church Rooms and is now incorporated in the Shannons Mill sheltered housing scheme.

MR JOHN O'NEILL AND FRIENDS, 1905

John O'Neill was a well known Tamworth butcher whose shop in Lichfield Street was on the site now occupied by the Norris Brothers' Garage. This postcard, taken in the yard at the back of The Boot Inn in Lichfield Street, shows O'Neill surrounded by a group of friends and customers. His dog, Spot, is sitting in front of the group.

THE MOAT HOUSE, TAMWORTH, 1904

The Moat House was built by William Comberford in 1572. During the royal visit to Tamworth in 1619, James I was lodged at the Castle and his son, the future Charles I, at The Moat House. Robert Woodings and his wife opened "a retired and eligible refuge for the unfortunate victims of insanity" here in 1815. When this postcard was published, The Moat House was the home of Edward Hollins, Chairman of Tamworth Magistrates. Since then the house has been a nursing home and then a restaurant. It is now vacant.

THE PEEL ARMS HOTEL, TAMWORTH, 1910

This inn on the corner of Market Street and Silver Street was originally The King's Arms. It was the principal coaching inn in the town with extensive stabling until the opening of the railway. Then its trade declined and about 1860 it was refurbished and renamed The Peel Arms. By 1910, when this postcard was published to advertise the Hotel, some of the stabling has been converted into garages. Notice that the Hotel's own omnibus met every train at Tamworth Station. The Hotel closed in 1989.

THE CASTLE HOTEL, TAMWORTH, 1905

There has been a licensed house on this site since 1635. In the eighteenth century it was famous for its mutton pies and fine ale. In 1838 it was badly damaged by fire which broke out during the night and trapped staff in the attics where they slept. Six female servants "were hurried from this time into eternity", to quote the monument raised to them in the churchyard. By 1905, when this postcard was produced for the convenience of those staying there, this was the leading hotel in the town.

TAMWORTH CASTLE LODGE, 1905

At the beginning of the nineteenth century Tamworth Castle was neglected and in poor repair. In 1810 the Marquis of Townsend, the owner of the Castle, carried out extensive repairs, laid out gardens and built this lodge at the entrance. The Townsend arms are over the archway. The other side of the Lodge, facing the Holloway, can be seen on the cover of this book. The Marmion arms are over the archway on that side. Note the fairy lights in the right foreground.

TAMWORTH CASTLE FROM THE AIR, 1939

The Castle was bought by Tamworth Corporation to commemorate Queen Victoria's Diamond Jubilee and opened to the public on 22nd May, 1899, when 5,000 people crowded into the Castle and its grounds. The land across the river was a tip until 1929 when the Corporation used 4,000 cubic yards of colliery spoil to raise it above flood level. It was then laid out as the Castle Pleasure Grounds.

THE BANDSTAND, TAMWORTH CASTLE, 1904

The Castle grounds were acquired by Tamworth Corporation in 1897 at the same time as the Castle and opened to the public two years later. The bandstand was erected in 1900 so that regular band concerts could be given to the public in the summer. This postcard shows the embankment before it was laid out in terraces and flower beds.

THE OAK ROOM, TAMWORTH CASTLE, 1904

This postcard shows the panelled Oak Room as it was when the Castle was first opened to the public. The room is dominated by the carved mantelpiece with a central panel bearing the arms of the Ferrers family and the motto "Only One". The large carved figures on either side are Sir John Ferrers and his wife and child. The smaller panels illustrate the legend of Venus and Adonis.

THE OPEN AIR BATHS, TAMWORTH, 1938

The open air bathing pool in the Castle Pleasure Grounds was opened in 1937. The barrier seen in this postcard separated the shallow water for young children, in the foreground, from the deeper water. The baths also included provision for sun-bathing on the flat roofs. The baths closed in 1989 when the Pleasure Grounds were re-developed.

TAMWORTH VOLUNTARY FIRE BRIGADE, 1920

In 1920 the Fire Brigade consisted of 14 volunteers who trained every other Thursday evening under Captain Woodcock. The Brigade owned a small hand pump, a Merryweather steam pump, a tender, and a two-wheel extending ladder - all shown on this postcard. The equipment was horse drawn but the Brigade had no horses. In case of fire the horses that pulled the Corporation refuse carts had to be hastily assembled. This postcard shows the Brigade and its equipment turned out for annual inspection in the Castle grounds. Not until 1926 did the Brigade take delivery of its first motor engine.

TAMWORTH MILLENARY PAGEANT, 1913

As part of the Millenary celebrations in 1913, a series of tableaux showing scenes from Tamworth's history were presented in the Castle grounds. The scene above shows Ethelfleda (Mrs F.H. Argyle) approving plans for a keep at Tamworth in 1913. Behind her stands her son, Athelstan (Dick Ford from Wigginton House). Other episodes showed St Editha and her nuns, the grant of the Castle to Robert de Marmion, Edward VI and the tanner of Tamworth, the visit of King James I, and the Civil War.

STEAM LAUNCH ON THE ANKER, 1905

An 1896 notice headed "Boating on the Anker" advertised "every description of boats for sale and hire at the Riverside Boat House, one minute walk from the railway station." The Boat House also advertised a fast steam launch for hire. On this postcard the launch can be seen approaching Lady Bridge.

THE BOAT HOUSE, TAMWORTH, 1932

This postcard shows a later boathouse, close to the junction of the Tame and Anker, from which rowing boats were hired out. Notice the ornamental wrought ironwork backs to the seats, often occupied by ladies, from which the boats were steered. The slipway has a slope at each side so that boats can be pulled out of the water more easily.

TAMWORTH CHAMBER OF COMMERCE OUTING, 1920

This char-a-banc outing organised by the Tamworth Chamber of Commerce was photographed outside Tamworth Castle before setting off. Outings like this to nearby beauty spots were popular in the 1920's when few individuals owned a motor car. The man sitting next to the driver was Mr Wilson; among the ladies in the second row are Miss Eva Rushton and Miss Page from Kettlebrook; Alfred Colbourne, the Tamworth auctioneer, and his wife are in the third row. Note the spare tyre behind the driver and the Birmingham "O" registration.

CANAL BRIDGES AT DRAYTON, 1912

These bridges were built over the Birmingham and Fazeley Canal at Drayton. The two towers have stairs leading to a foot bridge high enough for canal boats to pass beneath. There is also a swivel bridge by which horses and carts from the A4091 could reach the towpath and beyond.

DRAYTON MANOR, 1912

Drayton Manor was built by Robert Peel about 1790. His son, the second Robert Peel, whose statue stands in the centre of Tamworth, enlarged the house and landscaped the gardens. The fourth Robert Peel was a habitual gambler who frittered away the family fortune and was forced to put the house up for sale in 1925. It failed to find a buyer and was eventually demolished for the building materials.In 1949 the site was "a derelict rubbish dump" when it was bought by G.H.H. Bryant who developed it as a zoo and pleasure park.

THE LIBRARY, DRAYTON MANOR, 1905

Drayton Manor was furnished in the mid nineteenth century and remained largely unaltered in 1905. The Library was lit by bronze candelabra supported by storks, seen here on the right. The bookcases contained a famous collection of county histories and bound volumes of letters written to the Peels by Queen Victoria, Wellington and statesmen from every country. Over the bookcases can be seen busts of famous men of ancient times.

SWISS LODGE, DRAYTON MANOR PARK, 1910

Drayton Manor Park had three drives at the beginning of the present century. This lodge was at the Fazeley entrance. It was built about 1900 by the fourth Sir Robert Peel in Swiss style to remind his wife, Mercedes, daughter of Baron de Grafferied, of her home country. From the Lodge a fine avenue of oak and chestnut trees led past the Home Farm to Drayton Manor itself. The Lodge was demolished after World War Two.

THE TAMWORTH GREYHOUNDS, 1950

After the 1939-45 War the Tamworth Greyhound and Sports Stadium Ltd built a track at Deer Park on Watling Street between Fazeley and Mile Oak. Here they staged regular greyhound and speedway races. The glass topped cafeteria was, for a time, the centre of Saturday night entertainment in the area. This postcard shows the Tamworth "Hounds" speedway riders with Fred Yates on the right and Ted Gillespie third from the left. The stadium closed and the site was re-developed in the late 1950's.

FAZELEY, 1904

This postcard shows where the A4091 crossed the A5. The road to Tamworth lies beyond the White Lion on the right. Coleshill Street is on the left.

THE VICTORIA MEMORIAL HALL, FAZELEY, 1920

The Hall was presented to the parish in 1897 by James Eadie to mark Queen Victoria's Diamond Jubilee. Besides a large hall for concerts and public meetings there were smaller rooms and a library of 200 books. On the postcard on the opposite page the clock tower of the Hall can be seen to the left of the White Lion.

BONEHILL HOUSE, FAZELEY, 1906

Bonehill House was built in the nineteenth century for Sir Robert Peel's younger brother, Edmund, who had a calico printing works nearby. In 1906 it was owned by N.H. Everitt whose family can be seen posed in the garden for this postcard photographed by A.H. Weale.

TOLSON'S MILL, FAZELEY, 1912

William Tolson set up in business in Fazeley as a smallware manufacturer in 1854. His first mill was Peel's old cotton mill. In 1883 he built the steam powered mill, shown on this postcard, by the side of the Birmingham and Fazeley Canal. The impressive building is five storeys high and 29 bays long with a boiler house and chimney stack at the far end.

BROOK END, FAZELEY, 1921

Livinia Adkin, who took this photograph of Brook End, kept a newsagent's shop in Fazeley from about 1914 to 1930. She was also a photographer and published local postcards. This one can be dated 1921. The boy on the far right is Leslie Sidwells.

HOCKLEY ROAD, WILNECOTE, 1910

This postcard shows how rural Hockley Road was in 1910. The only clue to the exact location of the view is the stone retaining walls which can still be seen on either side of the road.

WATLING STREET, WILNECOTE, 1904

The view on this postcard is almost unrecognisable today because of improvements along Watling Street. On the right the sign of The Globe public house can be seen by the telegraph pole and this is the only building that remains on that side of the road. On the left the raised pavement has gone together with the shops facing onto it. Further away the shop with a double gable still stands. Today it is Atkins' newsagency and general stores

THE POST OFFICE, WILNECOTE, 1925

T. Hill's fruit and flower shop was also a post office in 1925 when this postcard was published. Note the letter box in the wall and the "Post Office" sign on the telegraph pole. Today all these buildings have been pulled down but the street sign "Smithy Lane" on the side of the shop shows where they used to be.

QUARRY HILL, WILNECOTE, 1925

This part of Wilnecote was not built up until just after 1900. Today all the houses on the right in this view have been pulled down but the houses on the left remain almost unaltered although "The Red Lion" has replaced the nearest house on that side of the road.

THE TOLL HOUSE, WILNECOTE, 1906

In the eighteenth and nineteenth centuries travellers paid a toll to travel along main roads like Watling Street. This house for the toll collector at Wilnecote stood close to where the Kettle Brook crosses Watling Street. There would have been a gate across the road to make sure everyone paid. By 1906, when this postcard was published, the toll had been discontinued and the gate removed.

TINKERS GREEN, WILNECOTE, 1905

Walk east along Tinkers Green Road, as it is called today. Where the road turns sharply south and Freasley Lane goes off to the left was a triangular space called Tinkers Green. In this view Freasley Lane and another cottage are just off-picture to the left. The families from the two cottages have turned out for the photographer.

THE MAIN ROAD, KETTLEBROOK, 1925
The houses in this part of Kettlebrook Road all date from the early 1900's. On the left is Albert Morrall's ladies hairdressing and tobacconist's shop opened in 1910.

SPRING COTTAGE, GLASCOTE, 1915

Spring Cottage, on the Glascote Road just east of Bolehall Viaduct, is the oldest building in this part of Glascote. The cottage, named after a spring that rose behind it, has been here for almost 300 years. In the eighteenth century it was occupied by the toll collector who collected a toll from all who travelled this road. Today, with a much altered front, it is occupied by Peel Interiors.

GLASCOTE ROAD, GLASCOTE, 1925

The local School Board built this school in the 1890's to provide for the evergrowing number of children in Glascote. Originally built as an all age boys' school it is now MacGregor County Junior School. The houses on the opposite side of the road were built in the early 1900's and have all been demolished in recent years.

BAMFORD STREET, GLASCOTE, 1925

Bamford Street takes its name from John Bamford, a local farmer. On the left is St George's Church built of local red brick in 1880. The tower with its curious saddle-back roof housed a single bell presented by Rev William MacGregor and his curates.

GLASCOTE ROAD, GLASCOTE, 1925

These houses all date from the early 1900's. The shop on the corner, now the Spar, was kept by Arthur Priestland, grocer, in 1925. Next to it is Cherry Cottage (1904) with its occupier barrowing a load of coal into his coal store, and Amelia Cottage (1907). Both houses have decorative date stones.

GLASCOTE, 1912

When A.W. Mills of Lichfield published this postcard in 1912 he titled it simply "Glascote". The exact location of the rural lane with its farm buildings is uncertain but Dumolo's Lane is most likely. In the early nineteenth century John Dumolo of Kettlebrook was a coal-master. Part of the lane that once led to his pit still exists and bears his name.

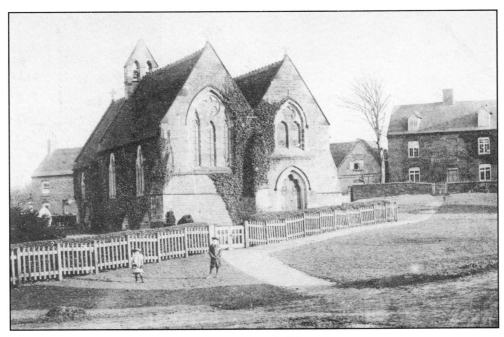

AMINGTON CHURCH, 1905

St Editha's Church was built in 1864 by C.H.W. a' Court Repington of Amington Hall. The east window has some notable Victorian stained glass. The house on the far right in this view was built in the eighteenth century but the house between it and the church (Fir Tree House) is much older.

AMINGTON HALL, 1904

Amington Hall is a handsome stone house built in the early nineteenth century and incorporating parts of a much older hall. The Hall belonged to the Repington family but in 1904 it was occupied by Sydney Fisher, Chairman of Fisher & Co, paper manufacturers, who was later killed when he fell through the floor at Kettlebrook paper mill.

OLD CROSSINGS, AMINGTON.

THE LEVEL CROSSING, AMINGTON

This postcard shows the level crossing at Amington with the signal box on the left and the crossing keeper's house in the centre. The track is a single up and a single down line. About 1902 the track was doubled to provide two lines in each direction and at the same time a bridge was built to carry the road to "The Pretty Pigs" over the railway line. The postcard was published in 1905 but it shows the crossing as it was before 1902.

WIGGINTON CHURCH, 1907

The small church of St Leonard was rebuilt in 1777 and the chancel added in 1862 by Mrs Robert Brown of Wigginton House. The chancel has been described as "faced with crazy paving".

WIGGINTON FROM THE HILL, 1909

Sydney Dewes, the Tamworth solicitor who lived at Wigginton Grange when he was a boy, described Wigginton as "a truly beautiful little village". He also recalled the Christmas concerts with refreshments on a "Parish Tray" provided by all the families and the outdoor party for the whole village every summer. This is one of very few postcards of the village.

THE CHEQUER, HOPWAS, 1937

At first glance "The Chequers" appears unchanged between 1937 and the present day. A closer look shows that the main entrance has been moved and that Truman's brewery has been replaced by Courage. The licencee in 1937 was Mrs Florence Fox.

HOPWAS CHURCH, 1906

When the old chapel of St John in the churchyard at Hopwas was demolished in 1881 this new church, dedicated to St Chad, was built on a different site north of the A51. The unusual building of red brick and timber has been described as "ingenious and entertaining". In 1906 the curate-in-charge was the Rev Alexander Stoddart.

THE PARSONAGE, HOPWAS, 1908

The parsonage on the Green dates from the 1840's when St John's Chapel was built in the small churchyard which still stands next to the house. The curate in charge lived here until the 1930's. The photographer has lined up some of the children who came to watch him with the old Dixons canal bridge behind them.

THE VILLAGE GREEN, HOPWAS, 1937

This postcard view, taken from near the Old Parsonage, shows the tree that stood on the Green before the present horse chestnut was planted. The pair of cottages have been here since the eighteenth century.

THE POST OFFICE AND STORES, SCHOOL LANE, HOPWAS, 1937
In 1937 the post-mistress was Miss Lizzie Wilson who also kept the Stores. This postcard and the one on the opposite page were both sold at her shop. Since 1937 the brick coach house on the right has been taken down and the house on the left given new windows and covered with pebble-dash, hiding the bricked up doorway clearly visible on the postcard.

SCHOOL LANE, HOPWAS, 1937

These neatly thatched seventeenth century cottages, across the road from the Post Office and Stores on the opposite page, are the oldest houses in the village,. On the far left is School House occupied in 1937 by Henry Hickin, schoolmaster and parish clerk. An inscribed stone on the front wall records that it was built by Thomas Barnes of London in 1717, "for the dwelling of a person to teach the children of this village English."

THE PUMPING STATION, HOPWAS, 1906

In the middle of the nineteenth century Tamworth had no piped water supply. Water came from private wells, from the rivers, and from water butts that collected rain water from roofs. Spring water for drinking was sold in the streets for a halfpenny a bucketful. In 1879 a bore hole was sunk at Hopwas and this pumping station built to supply piped water to the town. The resident engineer's house is on the right. The artist is W.G. Holt who drew several postcard views of Tamworth.